Question Your World

Creative Questions to Provoke Thought and Communication Between Youth and Adults

by

Takiya K. Akbar

authorHOUSE™

1663 LIBERTY DRIVE, SUITE 200
BLOOMINGTON, INDIANA 47403
(800) 839-8640
WWW.AUTHORHOUSE.COM

First published by AuthorHouse 12/10/04

ISBN: 1-4208-0348-4 (sc)

Printed in the United States of America
Bloomington, Indiana

This book is printed on acid-free paper.

With ALLAH'S Name, the Merciful Benefactor, the Merciful Redeemer

"If Allah is your helper none can overcome you and if He does not help you, who is there to help you? And on Allah let the believers rely" (3:160)

This Book is dedicated to my daughters Mizan, and Ruqayyah, and my younger sisters Samaiyah and Latifah.

About the Author

Takiya K. Akbar is a graduate of Lincoln University of Pennsylvania with a degree in Biology. The author's love for writing blossomed in High School with a school newspaper article on the popularity of Malcolm X among young people. Her other loves include science/medicine, fitness, foreign languages, tennis, financial independence and empowering the minds of youth. She resides in Maryland with her husband and two daughters.

A Word from the Author

You may be asking yourself how a book of questions can have a message. As a youth in an ever changing world you are constantly faced with a myriad of obstacles and questions. You'll have to come up with your own answers and your own meaning to the questions that you'll be faced with in life. Just as you will in this book. You will have questions about your morals, family, friends, school, the future, your ideals, and life aspirations. Questions abound all of our lives, from the simple to the complex; just as the questions in this book vary from simple to complex. Throughout all of life's trials and tribulations you should remain positive and focused. You should remain focused on the positive things in your life and the positive things to come, realizing that a greater burden than we have the strength to bear would not be placed on our shoulders. If it seems too tough then leave it up to the creator to handle.

In essence that is the message in this book of creative questions. Question and understand your existence and life purpose as someone special who will ultimately lead the world, with the creator's guidance and blessing. Enjoy being you even when it seems rough and impossible.

So, gather a group of your closest friends, your parents, siblings, classmates, or yourself, and have fun answering 365 questions that are guaranteed to make you think a little bit, laugh a little bit, and learn a lot about what you and others are thinking but, may not express to others. You may even be a little surprised by some of the answers. Feel free to write in the margins so that you can look back in a couple of years and see how your views have changed. Personalize this book as you try and predict how a friend or sibling might answer a question and then compare answers with that person. Take one question a day or as many as you like. Try and answer each question as far as you can. Don't settle for simple yes and no answers. Why cheat yourself out of learning as much as possible about yourself.

Attempt to go beyond the surface answer and look at your thinking from multiple angles. This may seem difficult at first, but with practice and assistance from others you'll get the hang of it and the process will become second nature. You can also use this book to formulate some questions of your own. **Make this book a personal vehicle to explore who you are and what you as a young person think.** How ever you choose to enjoy this book, just Enjoy!

YOUR
FUTURE
AHEAD

What do you like most about being a youth?

If you could shorten the number of teenager years, would you?

What does being a Muslim youth mean to you?

If you were to develop a criterion or standard for friendship, what would it be?

Who is more competitive, boys or girls, and why?

Takiya K. Akbar

If you were chosen to be a counselor for a youth group, what issues would you focus on and how would you address them?

Where do you see your friends in 10 years?

What is the one thing most teenagers dislike?

How are youth most misunderstood?

What would you say is the one thing most youth love?

What type of friend would others say you are?

If you wanted to give a speech tomorrow to your class what topic would you speak on?

Can you name one person your age that you admire for something good he/she has done?

If your friends wanted to surprise you with a gift, what would be the best choice?

How would you change the way youth treat one another?

What are 5 qualities to have in a good friend?

What are some of the hardest things about being a Muslim?

If you and your friends started your own language what would you call it and how would it sound?

What do you think your friends will be doing in 5 years?

If you could pick 2 friends to be your college roommates, who would they be?

If you could predict which one of your friends will get married first, who would you say, why?

If you could be a mentor to younger kids, what types of things would you mentor on?

If you were in charge of the youth activities at your house of worship, what activities would you plan?

Which one of your friends has the worst taste in food?

If you wanted to create a summer camp, what activities would you include?

What would your friends say that you have the best taste in?

If it was up to you, what age would you allow youth to drive?

What would you say is the best part of puberty?

What's the worst thing about puberty?

If you were to predict what your generation will contribute to the world, what would you say?

If you and your friends were lost in the woods, who amongst you could successfully lead the group to safety?

If you were the leader of all religious groups on earth what kind of things would you change or implement?

If you could change one physical thing about yourself, what would it be and why?

What advice would you give youth whose parents have recently divorced?

In what ways do people use your age to treat you younger than you are?

What's the most wasteful thing your friends spend their money on?

f you were the principal of your school or one month, what changes would you make?

f you had to identify the best and worst things about home schooling, what would you say?

f you had a choice to be home schooled or taught in public school, which would you choose?

f you could predict who in your class would be the biggest success in life, who would you say?

f you could choose to give one teacher a raise, who would it be and how much would you give her?

Would you rather your mom teach you or a stranger, why?

If you could attend school anywhere in the world, where would you go?

If you could have any restaurant in your school which would you choose?

If you could plan an end of the year field trip, where would you go?

If there was a gold medal for teaching which one of you teachers would receive it?

If you were asked to remove one class period from your school schedule, which would be removed?

I f you could make your fantasy class schedule, what would it look like?

W hat new rules would you implement in your school, why?

W hich school rules would you eliminate, why?

D id you know that in some countries, attending school is against the law?

I f you had to eat one type of food for lunch for the rest of the school year, what would it be?

If you had to stay in one grade for life, which would you choose, why?

Have you ever received a grade good/bad that you felt you didn't deserve?

If you could hangout after school in one place, where would it be and who would be there?

If you could have a celebrity guest at your graduation, who would you choose?

If you could decorate your school locker anyway you liked, what would it look like?

If you could teach one school subject, which would you choose?

If you could have a full scholarship to attend any university, where would you go?

Which school subject do you find the least useful?

What are you looking forward to doing after graduation?

What habit of one of your classmates do you wish you could change?

If you could go to school at night instead of in the day, would you do this?

If you had a choice of wearing a uniform or not, which would you choose?

How would you modify your school uniform?

If you could change the time that you had to be in school, what would it be?

How would you design a gymnasium or athletic center for your school?

If you could graduate one year early, but have to attend school all year round, would you do it?

If you were asked to rename your school, what would you call it?

Upon graduating, what honors would you like to earn?

If you could have anyone young or old speak at your graduation, who would it be, why?

What's the most valuable lesson you've learned from a teacher?

What's the most valuable lesson you've shared with someone else?

If you were given the choice to die right now and be granted paradise or live out the rest of your life, which would you choose, why?

How would you change the way your parents act toward you?

If your religious affiliation in America went to war tomorrow, what would your family do?

If your parents were you age today what type of youth would they be?

If there is one thing you wouldn't want your parents to know, what would it be?

If there is one thing that you and your parents agree least on, what is it and why?

If you could send your parents to college to study a subject of your choice, what subject would you choose?

What's the one thing that you and your parents agree most on?

If you could tell your parents one thing that they may not know about you, what would you say?

If you could stop a war that would kill many, but in the process you would loose a relative, would you stop the war?

If you had to live with someone besides your parents or guardian who would it be?

Where do you see yourself and your family in 10 years?

If you could switch parents for a day, whose parents would you switch with?

If your parents allowed you to stay outside for as long as you wanted, how long would you stay?

If you could choose a college major for your siblings, what would it be?

What's the funniest thing your parents have ever said or done to you?

If you could change one way your parents act in front of your friends, what would it be?

What's the most unfair punishment you've ever received from your parents?

If you could redecorate your parent's bedroom, what would you change?

If you found out that you were switched at birth, how would your life change?

What types of friends would your parents pick for you?

I f you could change you parent's names what would you change them to?

I f your parents were to take in a foster child with a troubled background, what would you say or do?

I f your parents were to pick your career, what would they pick?

I f your parents knew someone who could get you accepted into college without you applying, what would you want them to do?

I f you could switch birth order with your a sibling, would you do it and how would it change your life?

What do you consider a normal family life and do you have one?

If you had a twin for a week, what would you do together?

If you were watching a trouble child, how would you tell the parents that you no longer wanted to watch their child?

If your parents could spend more time doing one thing with you, what would you want it to be?

If you and a parent switched bodies for a day, what types of situations would you face?

What topic do you feel more comfortable talking about with friends than your parents?

What do you love most about your parents?

What qualities of your parents would you most like to have?

If you and your friends or siblings could start a fashion trend, what would it be?

If you were a kid when your parents were kids, do you think that you would hang out together?

DON'T DO DRUGS

If your parents were going to punish you by making you do a chore, which would they pick?

Which season best describes your family members and yourself?

If you could pick new parents, how would your new parents differ from your existing parents?

If you were asked to design a family website how would it look; what pictures and stories would you share?

What is the most valuable lesson you've learned so far from your parents?

I f you could change your parent's profession to anything you wanted, what would you pick?

I f your parents were going to punish you by taking away something dear to you, what would be most effective?

I f you could change the current age of your parents to make them younger or older, which would you choose, why?

W hat has been your most memorable family vacation or outing thus far?

I f you could keep only one picture of your family which one would you choose and why?

If you could spend the day with anyone from your family's history, whom would you choose?

What characteristics of your mom do you see in yourself?

What characteristics of your dad do you see in yourself?

If you could do something very special for your parents without spending money, what would you do?

If your parents died tomorrow what about them would you miss the most?

What acts of Sadaqah (charitable deed) have you done this week?

If you were to choose one of the Prophet's wives to pattern your life after, who would you pick, why?

If you were confused about something related to your religion, who would you talk with?

What's the difference between "blind following" and "conscious following"?

If any of the creator's prophets were alive today, what do you think they would say about this world?

What are 5 qualifications of a good religious leader?

If you could choose any person to be the religious leader of over your house of worship, who would you choose?

What is your plan for getting into paradise?

What types of activities and programs would attract more youth to your house of worship?

What is your ideal wife or husband?

Knowing the creator sees your every move, how has that shaped your choices in life?

If you could be one of the Prophet's companions which one would you be and why?

What's the biggest misunderstanding about your religious group?

Did you make all of your prayers yesterday?

What act of Sadaqah (charitable deed) have you done today?

What's the difference between Zakat and Sadaqah?

What are the main differences between Muslims and Christians?

Did you know that you can receive blessings by waking others up for prayer?

What challenges do you face the most as a Muslim today?

What's the most recent lesson that you've learned while reading the Qur'an or Holy book?

Do you think that Muslims are allowed to be wealthy?

If someone challenged you to give 5 examples of the creators power, what would you say?

If you wanted to prove to someone that your religion is the one for them, what would you say?

As a Muslim, what do you feel should be one of your biggest contributions to society?

What's your most favorite Surah (chapter) in the Qur'an?

Do you think about the consequences of your daily actions and how your actions can affect your community?

If you could change one thing about your house of worship, what would it be?

How would you handle someone who criticized your religion?

If you could have a conversation with the two angels that write down your deeds, what would you say?

Do you feel that your religious group should know about and respect other religions?

What would you ask the creator to grant you more of?

Which movie about your religious group, angers you the most, why?

If your best friend asked for your advice on how to be a better person, what would you say?

If the world was destined to end in 7 days, what would you do to prepare for the day of judgment?

Why were people created?

I f there existed an Islamic University in the U.S. would you attend and what would you study?

I f you could pray for one celebrity to take their Shahadah (declaration of faith), who would it be and why?

H ow has your perception of war changed over the years?

W hat ways do you think that you or your peers compromise your religion?

C an you name 5 ways to make your jinn submit or make Sajdah (prostration)?

If the Prophet Muhammad (p.b.u.h.) hung out with you for a week, what do you think he would say about your life?

Is there a downside to being raised a Muslim?

What are the similarities of Muslims and Christians?

How do you envision Paradise and is there such a thing as paradise on earth?

How do you envision Hell Fire and is there such a thing as Hell on earth?

What benefits have you gained by being raised as a Muslim?

What's your best Eid memory or religious holiday memory?

If you could meet any one in history who would you choose?

What's the best way that you can contribute to the world?

If you could call anyone in the world and talk for free for an hour, who would you call?

If you met a youth who was deaf or blind, how would you communicate?

What was the silliest thing you've done to impress someone important to you?

If you could remove certain material from the internet, what would you remove?

If you were chosen to be the president of a country, which country would you choose, and how would you rule?

If you could rename one state, what would it be called?

I f you had to choose between sight or hearing which would you choose, why?

I f you were asked to write a play about anything you wanted, what would it be about?

I f you could be as physically strong as one person, who would it be?

I f you could stick up for one world cause, what would it be?

I f you could star in your own TV show what would you call it and what would it be about?

If you could have World Peace or cure World Hunger which would you choose, why?

If you had 24 hrs to spend 1 million dollars how would you do it?

What are the 3 most positive things you could say about a close friend?

How would you propose to repair the hole in the ozone layer above the earth?

What's the best dinner you've ever had?

What type of radio show would you produce if given the chance?

What's the best web site you've ever seen?

What bugs you the most about your government?

If you could change 3 things about the world, what would they be?

What's the stupidest thing you've come across on the internet?

f you could design a car anyway you wanted,
how would it look?

f you could be paid to do one thing special,
what would it be?

f you compared your education to others,
do you feel that your education is better or
worst, why?

f you could win any one award, which one
would you want to win?

f you were on a deserted Island, what 3 items
would you want with you?

If you could host your own TV show what would you talk about?

What's the worst dinner you've ever had?

What's the silliest thing you've ever spent money for?

What's the difference between a boy and a man?

What's the difference between girl and a woman?

Which one of your friend's talents do you wish that you had?

Why was the world created with different ethnicities, cultures, customs and languages?

If you could extract 5 words from the English language which would you choose?

If you were asked to create 3 new words to be added to the dictionary, what would they be?

Do you feel that society views women negatively, why?

If you could read the mind of one person, who would it be?

If you could have a dinner party with 3 people from history, who would you choose?

What single moment in history would you like to relive or witness if given the chance?

I f you could spend one hour a day talking on the phone with one world leader, who would it be?

I f you could ban one thing in the world, what would it be?

I f you could bring back one extinct species, which would you choose?

I f you could witness one war in history which would you choose and why?

I f you could be known for the cure of one disease past or present, which would you choose?

I f you could choose to have one season a year without any environmental problems, which would you choose?

I f you were an animal, which would you be, why?

I f you could decorate your room to look like a specific country, which would you choose?

I f you had to leave home right this moment, what one thing would you take with you (besides money)?

I f you had to spend a day as your pet, what do you think you would experience?

If you could create a career that no one else has thought of, what would it be?

If you were to spend 5 hrs a week volunteering, where would you volunteer?

What lessons about your life have you learned so far?

If given an opportunity would you want to take a trip into outer space?

If you could go on a $500 shopping spree in any store, where would you go?

What negative influences from TV can you detect in yourself?

If you were abandoned on an island, what would you do to survive?

What type of part-time business could you create for yourself?

If you owned a movie theater what types of movies would you show?

If you could blink your eyes and have one person apologize for doing something wrong, who would it be?

If you were asked to create a new bubble gum flavor what would it be?

If you could own one internet company that exists today, which would you choose?

If you were confined to your home for 30 days, what would you do during this time?

What's your dream summer job?

If you were to make a commercial for one product in your refrigerator, what would you choose and what would you do?

I f you were approached by a weird or odd person while waiting for a bus, how would you respond?

I f you could deliver a pizza to someone famous, who would it be?

I f you could rent a car right now, where would you want to go?

I f you could buy your dream home, how many rooms would it have?

W hat would be your dream car to design and manufacture?

If you had to wear the same outfit everyday for a month, which outfit would you choose?

If you were a journalist for a week, what issues would you write about?

If you didn't have a TV, computer, telephone, or car, what would you do to have fun?

If you could bring one person with you on a trip to the moon, who would it be?

Would you rather own your own business and make $30,000 a year or work for someone else making $80,000 a year?

I f you and 7 guests were given a personal jet for a week where would you visit, and who would you take?

W hat is your all time favorite candy, new or old?

I f you were to change the lyrics to your favorite song, what would it sound like?

W hich toy from your childhood gives you the most memories?

I f you could make one object in the world larger or smaller, what object would you choose and how would you change it?

What is the one place on earth that you never want to visit, why?

If you were asked to be amongst the first inhabitants of a new planet, would you go?

If you were the owner of a hair shop for women or men, what would you name it?

What's one of your favorite books?

If you were in control of television, what programs would you broadcast?

Takiya K. Akbar

If you could master a sport or martial art which would you choose?

If you could wake up tomorrow and be fluent in three languages, which would you choose and why?

What 3 slang words are you most tired of hearing?

What 3 things would you give someone homeless?

If you volunteered as a Big Brother or Sister, what values would you try to teach other youth?

I f you were to propose one solution to the Middle East conflict, what would it be?

I f you could accomplish one thing in life, what would it be, why?

I f a friend was in trouble with the law, would you tell your parents?

I f a friend confided in you that he/she was planning to run away, what would you do?

f you witnessed the physical abuse of a parent, who would you ask help from?

f someone at school was being harassed, would you step in to help the person?

f you were wrongfully accused of doing something, how would you prove your innocence?

f you had access to the answers to a test would you look at them?

I f you found a brown bag filled with $500, what would you do?

I f you were given one million dollars to establish a foundation or charity, what cause would you choose?

W hat would you do if a friend asked for your answers to a test?

D o you think that cloning should exist, why?

I f your best friend was in trouble and asked you to lie about it, what would you do?

I f you had to lie about your age to get into a movie, would you?

I f you had a choice between marrying a righteous (only) person or a physically attractive (only) person, who would you choose, why?

I f you were asked to play a game that you knew in your heart was wrong, but all your friends wanted you to play, would you?

f you were invisible for 24 hrs, what would you do?

f you wanted to raise $500 for charity, what types of things would you do?

f you could read one person's email (with his/her permission) whose would you choose?

f your identical twin asked you to take an exam for him/her, would you?

f you walked into a room and a group of people were making fun of your friend, what would you do or say?

If you had to give up a personal freedom to save the life of someone else, which freedom would you give up?

If you could prevent slavery, the Middle East conflict, or the two World Wars, which would you prevent and why?

Have you ever signed your mom or dad's name on a document without their knowledge? How did you feel about that?

Have you ever broken something in your or a relative's home and allowed someone else to be blamed for it?

I f you've ever allowed someone else to be blamed for your mistake, how did your conscience feel afterwards?

I s it possible to have too much of a good thing?

W hat do you never leave the house without, no matter what?

W hat is the worst thing you've experienced in your life?

I f you found out that you weren't accepted into college, what would you do?

I f you knew you would die tomorrow, how would you live today?

I f you knew that you were going to live for only 50 years, how would you live today?

W hose point of view do you wish you understood better?

I f you could name one thing you wish people knew about you what would it be?

I f you could keep one thing secret about you, what would it be?

What would be the most embarrassing thing that could happen to you in public?

If you woke up and you were 2 feet taller, how would your life change?

If you were 2 feet shorter tomorrow, how would your life change?

If you could live for 200 years, would you want to?

What are the three most important goals in your life?

If you had to make the world either larger or smaller which would you choose?

If you could be the smartest person, but suffer from severe acne or be the dumbest person with perfect skin, which would you choose?

If you could wake up tomorrow and be any age, which age would you choose, why?

What other planet would you like to visit, if given the chance?

What's the hardest thing you've ever had to tell someone ?

If you had to get married tomorrow or you would never be able to get married, would you get married?

If you felt that you were disrespected by a teacher how would you handle the situation?

What's the most disgusting thing you've done, that no one knows about?

What accomplishments has your generation contributed to society?

What's the best way you've contributed to your community?

If you could refine one skill of yours, what would it be?

If your country went to war tomorrow, how would your life change?

If your favorite musical artist asked you to design an upcoming CD cover, how would it look?

If you died tomorrow, what would you want people to say about you in their prayers?

What's the worst way to die that you could imagine?

If you were going to die tomorrow, how would you want to die?

What's one characteristic about yourself that you would like to change?

What's the best part of your personality?

What would you do if a friend "borrowed" a paper that you wrote and turned it in as her assignment?

If you were to write a song about your life, how would it sound?

How would your life change if you were a different race?

How would your life change if you were from a different culture?

What forms of peer pressure have you encountered since Sept. 11, 2001?

Have you ever felt so angry that you wanted to hit something or someone, How did you calm yourself down?

If someone wrote a book about your life, what would the last chapter say?

What would your life be like if you were suddenly homeless tomorrow?

What about your life makes you happy?

What about your life makes you mad?

What's the most difficult personal problem that you've overcome?

If you could erase one thing that you did yesterday what would it be?

What does being successful mean to you?

What does being unsuccessful mean to you?

What has been the scariest thing that you've ever encountered?

What steps are necessary to live a financially independent life?

Are you a leader or follower amongst your group of friends?

Who in your life influences you the most?

If you could be on an Olympic team, which sport would you represent?

What's the most uncomfortable thing you've experienced in your life so far?

If you were to change your name, what would it be?

What's the biggest change in your life since one year ago?

What mistakes in life (so far) have you made that you regret?

At what age would you consider yourself a grown-up?

Which of your friends has the best taste in movies?

At what age would you be considered old?

If you were fired from a job because, you were a Muslim what would you do?

If you were told that you were hired for a summer job only because of your religion, how would you respond?

How would you propose to stop violence against women?

When you look in the mirror do you see a beautiful or handsome person?

How do you think your life would change if you were eighteen right now?

How would you describe yourself in one word?

Would you rather live life as a 5 year old or a 75 year old?

If you spoke with a therapist in private, what personal concerns would you talk about?

If you could create a board game based on your life, what would it be titled and how would you play it?

Who's the one person under thirty that you trust the most?

Who is the one person over thirty that you trust the most?

If you could be a character in a book, which book and character would you choose?

What's the worst thing someone could do to betray your trust?

What mistake of the past would you not want your generation to repeat?

What would you like to see happen in your life within 10 years?

Which song past or present best describes your life?

What's one thing that you would like to master by the time you are 18?

If you were allowed to have one tragedy in life prevented, which would you choose and why?

Where do you go when you need peace and time to think?

(HAPPINESS)

"THINK ABOUT THIS"

This book will challenge the thinking of today's youth requiring them to use their mind power and creator given intellect to decipher the world around them. The time never existed when mediocre thinking was accepted by successful people. We can not start now. In this book **Takiya Akbar** offers youth, parents and educators a vehicle for establishing and continuing healthy dialogue, self-discovery and critical thinking opportunities through the daily use of simple and complex questions.

Do you think about the consequences of your daily actions and how they can affect your community?

If you could prevent the African-American Slavery experience, the Middle East Conflict, or the two World Wars, which would you prevent and why?